The Big Book of Baby Names 2022

By Jane Summers

A

Aadam
Aadhya
Aadil
Aadya
Aahana
Aahil
Aaleyah
Aaliyah
Aanya
Aarav
Aariz
Aarna
Aarohi
Aaron
Aarush
Aarya
Aaryan
Aavya
Aayan
Aayush
Abalone
Abbas
Abbey

Abbie
Abbigail
Abby
Abbygail
Abdiel
Abdirahman
Abdul
Abdullah
Abdullahi
Abdulrahman
Abdur
Abdurrahman
Abe
Abel
Abelard
Abelia
Aberforth
Abigail
Abigale
Abilene
Abina
Abner
Abraham
Abram
Abriella
Abrielle
Abril

Abu	Adalynn
Abubakar	Adalynne
Abygail	Adam
Acacia	Adamaris
Acacio	Adan
Acacius	Addalyn
Acadia	Addax
Acantha	Addelyn
Ace	Addilyn
Acedia	Addilynn
Acer	Addison
Achilles	Addisyn
Acker	Addyson
Ackley	Adela
Acton	Adelaida
Ada	Adelaide
Adair	Adelard
Adalardo	Adelbert
Adalee	Adele
Adalia	Adelia
Adalie	Adelin
Adalina	Adelina
Adalind	Adeline
Adaline	Adelio
Adaly	Adelle
Adalyn	Adelyn
Adalyne	Adelyne

Adelynn	Adrianna
Adelynne	Adriano
Adem	Adriatic
Aden	Adriel
Aderyn	Adrien
Adesina	Adrienne
Adetokunbo	Advika
Adger	Adyan
Adhya	Adyn
Adia	Aegle
Adil	Aella
Adilene	Aeneas
Adin	Aengus
Adina	Aeon
Adira	Aerin
Aditi	Aeris
Aditya	Aerith
Adlai	Aero
Adler	Aerolynn
Adley	Aeson
Admon	Afia
Adnan	Afonso
Adolfo	Afric
Adolph	Africa
Adonis	Afsaneh
Adrian	Afsha
Adriana	Afton

Agamemnon	Ailany
Agatha	Ailbhe
Agathon	Ailee
Aglaia	Aileen
Aglaze	Ailidh
Agnes	Ailill
Agrippina	Ailis
Agrona	Ailsa
Agustin	Ailyn
Ahana	Aimee
Ahearn	Aimi
Ahern	Aimilios
Ahmad	Aina
Ahmed	Aine
Ahmir	Aingeal
Ai	Ainhoa
Aida	Ainsley
Aidan	Aira
Aiden	Airell
Aidric	Airic
Aife	Airyck
Aigneis	Aisha
Aika	Aislinn
Aiken	Aislynn
Aiko	Aitana
Aila	Aithne
Ailani	Aiya

Aiyana	Alameda
Aiyanna	Alamo
Aiza	Alan
Ajax	Alana
Ajay	Alanah
Akako	Alane
Akane	Alani
Akasuki	Alanna
Akela	Alannah
Akemi	Alanson
Aki	Alaric
Akihiko	Alastair
Akihiro	Alastrina
Akiko	Alastrine
Akina	Alastriona
Akira	Alaya
Akita	Alayah
Aksel	Alayla
Akshara	Alayna
Al	Alba
Alaa	Albedo
Alabaster	Alberic
Aladdin	Albert
Alaia	Alberta
Alain	Alberto
Alaina	Albie
Alaiya	Albina

Albion

Albus

Alby

Alcaeus

Alcott

Alda

Alden

Alder

Aldo

Aldric

Aldrich

Aleah

Alec

Aled

Aleeah

Aleen

Aleena

Aleenah

Aleia

Alejandra

Alejandro

Aleksander

Aleksandra

Aleksandrina

Alena

Alene

Aleph

Aleron

Alessa

Alessandra

Alessandro

Alessia

Alessio

Alethea

Aletris

Alex

Alexa

Alexander

Alexandra

Alexandre

Alexandria

Alexandru

Alexi

Alexia

Alexis

Alexsus

Alexxa

Alexzander

Aleyah

Aleyda

Aleydis

Aleyna

Aleyza

Alfie

Alfie-james
Alfie-lee
Alfonso
Alford
Alfred
Alfredo
Algernon
Ali
Alia
Aliah
Aliana
Alianna
Alibeth
Alice
Alicia
Alienor
Alijah
Alima
Alina
Alinah
Aline
Alinna
Alisa
Alisha
Alison
Alissa
Alisson

Alistair
Alivia
Aliya
Aliyah
Aliyana
Aliza
Alizae
Alizah
Alizay
Alize
Allan
Allard
Allegra
Allen
Allena
Allene
Allie
Allison
Allisson
Allston
Allura
Ally
Allyn
Allyson
Alma
Almeda
Almera

Almond

Aloe

Alohi

Alois

Alok

Alon

Alondra

Alonso

Alonzo

Alora

Aloysius

Alpha

Alphaeus

Alpine

Alta

Altagracia

Altair

Althaea

Althea

Althia

Alton

Alun

Alvaro

Alvena

Alvertos

Alvia

Alvin

Alvina

Alviria

Alwyn

Alya

Alyah

Alyana

Alyanna

Alycia

Alyna

Alynna

Alys

Alyson

Alyssa

Alysson

Alyvia

Amaan

Amabel

Amachi

Amadeus

Amado

Amador

Amaia

Amairani

Amairany

Amal

Amalia

Aman

Amanda	— Amelia
Amani	Amelie
Amapola	Amen
Amar	America
Amara	Americo
Amarah	Americus
Amaranth	Amerie
Amarantha	Amethyst
Amari	Ami
Amariah	Amia
Amarie	Amiah
Amarion	Amias
Amaris	Amida
Amaryllis	Amie
Amasa	Amilia
Amaterasu	Amin
Amaya	Amina
Amayah	Aminah
Ambar	Amir
Amber	Amira
Amberline	Amirah
Amberly	Amiya
Amboree	Amiyah
Ambretta	Ammar
Ambrose	Ammon
Ameer	Amor
Ameera	Amora

Amory	Analiyah
Amos	Analy
Amoura	Anant
Amphitrite	Ananya
Amy	Anas
An	Anastasia
Ana	Anastasius
Anabel	Anat
Anabella	Anatase
Anabelle	Anatole
Anacletus	Anatolia
Anafa	Anaya
Anahi	Anayah
Anahit	Anders
Anahita	Anderson
Anais	Andi
Anaisha	Andie
Anaiya	Andraste
Anaiyah	Andre
Anakin	Andrea
Analeah	Andreas
Analee	Andrei
Anali	Andres
Analia	Andrew
Analiah	Androcles
Analisa	Andromeda
Analise	Andy

Anemone	Anka
Anessa	Ann
Anezka	Ann/e
Angel	Anna
Angela	Annabel
Angelia	Annabell
Angelica	Annabella
Angelie	Annabelle
Angelina	Annabeth
Angeline	Annaisha
Angelique	Annaleah
Angelo	Annalee
Anghus	Annalia
Angie	Annalie
Angus	Annaliese
Ani	Annalisa
Ania	Annalise
Anika	Annamarie
Anisa	Annan
Anise	Anne
Anish	Annelise
Anisha	Annette
Anissa	Annie
Anita	Annika
Aniya	Annwfn
Aniyah	Annwn
Anjali	Anny

Annya	Anzu
Ansel	Aod
Anselm	Aodh
Ansgar	Aodhan
Ansh	Aoife
Ansley	Aonghus
Anson	Ap Owen
Anthea	Apastron
Anthony	Aphelion
Antigone	Aphria
Antipas	Aphrodite
Antoine	Apollo
Antoinette	Apollonia
Anton	Apostolos
Antonella	Apple
Antoni	April
Antonia	Aquila
Antonio	Aquilina
Antony	Ara
Antwan	Arabella
Anuhea	Arabelle
Anvi	Araceli
Anvika	Aracely
Anwell	Aragorn
Anwyl	Arakan
Anya	Araluen
Anyon	Aram

Araminta	Aretha
Aramis	Argyle
Aran	Arham
Arantxa	Ari
Arantza	Aria
Aranza	Ariadna
Arata	Ariadne
Arawn	Ariah
Araya	Arian
Araylia	Ariana
Arbor	Arianna
Arcadia	Arianny
Arcadio	Ariany
Archer	Aribella
Archibald	Aric
Archie	Arie
Ardell	Ariel
Ardelle	Ariela
Arden	Ariella
Ardena	Arielle
Ardene	Arienh
Ardra	Aries
Arela	Arild
Areli	Arina
Arella	Aris
Arely	Arisbeth
Ares	Arisu

Ariya	Armando
Ariyah	Armani
Arizbeth	Armstrong
Arjan	Arnas
Arjun	Arnav
Arkin	Arnold
Arlan	Arnost
Arlana	Aron
Arland	Arran
Arledge	Arron
Arleen	Arrow
Arleigh	Arroyo
Arlen	Art
Arlene	Artair
Arlet	Arte
Arleta	Artek
Arleth	Artemis
Arlett	Arthur
Arlette	Artie
Arley	Artis
Arlin	Arto
Arlina	Artur
Arline	Arturo
Arlo	Arty
Arlyn	Arun
Armaan	Arundel
Arman	Arvid

Arwen	Asto
Arya	Astri
Aryan	Asuka
Aryana	Atarah
Aryanna	Athelstan
Asa	Athena
Asami	Atlantic
Asees	Atlas
Ash	Atreus
Asha	Atria
Ashanti	Atsushi
Ashby	Atticus
Asher	Attie
Ashley	Atty
Ashly	Atur
Ashlyn	Atziri
Ashlynn	Au
Ashton	Aubree
Ashwin	Aubrey
Asia	Aubri
Asiya	Aubriana
Asma	Aubrianna
Aspen	Aubrie
Asra	Aubriella
Assumpta	Aubrielle
Aster	Auburn
Asteria	Audelia

Auden	Avalyn
Audra	Avalynn
Audree	Avani
Audrey	Aveline
Audriana	Averi
Audrianna	Averie
Audrie	Averill
Audrina	Avery
August	Aviana
Augusta	Avianna
Augustine	Avigail
Augustus	Avis
Auk	Aviva
Aulani	Avleen
Aura	Avneet
Aurelia	Avni
Aurelio	Avocet
Aurelius	Avon
Aurora	Avonlea
Austen	Avril
Austin	Avyanna
Austin / Austen	Awarnach
Austyn	Awnan
Autumn	Axel
Ava	Axl
Avah	Axton
Avalon	Aya

Ayaan
Ayah
Ayaka
Ayako
Ayame
Ayan
Ayana
Ayanna
Ayano
Ayden
Aydin
Ayesha
Ayla
Aylani
Ayleen
Aylen
Aylin
Ayman
Ayomide
Ayoub
Ayra
Ayrton
Ayub
Ayumi
Ayush
Ayva
Ayvah

Aza
Azaan
Azalea
Azami
Azaria
Azariah
Azeneth
Aziel
Azrael
Azucena
Azul
Azumi
Azure

B

Baby
Baiji
Baikal
Bailee
Bailey
Baird
Bairrfhionn
Baker
Bali
Ballard
Balsam
Bancroft
Banks
Bannon
Banyan
Baptiste
Barbara
Barbary
Barclay
Bard
Barden
Bardon
Barkley
Barley
Barnaby
Barnett
Barney
Barra
Barracuda
Barrett
Barrie
Barry
Bartholomew
Bartlomiej
Bartosz
Basil
Bast
Baxter
Bay
Bayard
Baylee
Baylor
Bayo
Bayou
Bayre
Beacan
Beach
Beacher
Bean
Bear

Bearacb
Bearcban
Beardsley
Beatha
Beatrice
Beatrix
Beatriz
Beau
Becan
Beck
Beckett
Beckham
Bede
Bedelia
Bedrich
Bedwyr
Beech
Begonia
Bela
Belarius
Beldon
Belen
Belinda
Bella
Belladonna
Bellamy
Bellarose

Bellatrix
Belle
Bellerose
Belva
Ben
Benas
Bendigeidfran
Benedict
Bénédicta
Benes
Benicio
Benita
Benito
Benjamin
Bennett
Bennie
Benny
Beno
Benoit
Benson
Bente
Bentlee
Bentley
Berenice
Bergamot
Bergen
Berit

Berkeley	Bibia
Berkley	Bijou
Berlin	Bilal
Bernadette	Bill
Bernard	Billie
Bernardo	Billy
Bernice	Billy/Billie
Berry	Bina
Berta	Birch
Bertie	Birdie
Beryl	Birgit
Bessie	Birk
Beta	Birkita
Betania	Birte
Betha	Bjarki
– Bethany	Björk
Betony	Bjorn
Betsy	Blaine
Bettany	Blainey
Betty	Blair
Bevan	Blaire
Beverly	Blaise
Bevin	Blake
Bevyn	Blakeley
Bexley	Blakely
Bianca	Blanca
Bianka	Blanche

Blanchefleur	Bohdan
Blane	Bohumil
Blayke	Bohumir
Blayne	Bohuslav
Blayney	Bojan
Blaze	Bojanek
Blazej	Bojek
Blessing	Bojik
Blizzard	Bolek
Blodwen	Boleslav
Bloom	Bolide
Blossom	Bonnie
Blue	Bonsai
Bluebell	Booker
Blythe	Boone
Bo	Booth
Boaz	Borden
Bobbie	Borivoj
Bobby	Borys
Bobby / Bobbie	Boston
Bode	Botan
Boden	Boulder
Bodhi	Bovra
Bodie	Bovrek
Body	Bovrik
Bogdan	Bovza
Bogdashka	Bovzek

Bowden
Bowdyn
Bowen
Bowie
Bowyn
Boyd
Boyden
Boynton
Bozidar
Brad
Braden
Bradford
Bradley
Bradly
Brady
Braeden
Braelyn
Braelynn
Braiden
Bramble
Bran
Branch
Brandan
Branden
Brandon
Brangaine
Branik

Branislav
Brann
Branson
Brant
Brantley
Branwen
Brarn
Brasil
Bratislav
Braxton
Bray
Brayan
Brayden
Braydon
Braylee
Braylen
Braylon
Brazil
Brea
Breanainn
Breandan
Breanna
Breccia
Brecken
Bredon
Bree
Breeda

Breeze	Brian
Breezie	Briana
Breezy	Briann
Brencis	Brianna
Brenda	Briannah
Brendan	Brianne
Brenden	Briannon
Brendon	Briano
Brendt	Briant
Brenna	Briar
Brennan	Brice
Brennen	Bricriu
Brent	Brid
Brenten	Bride
Brentley	Bridger
Brently	Bridget
Brenton	Bridgette
Breslin	Bridie
Bressal	Briella
Bret	Brielle
Bretislav	Brien
Brett	Brienna
Bretta	Brienne
Brewster	Brietta
Bria	Briggs
Briac	Brigham
Briallen	Brighid

Brighton
Brigid
Brigitta
Brigitte
Brina
Brinicle
Brinley
Brion
Briony
Brisa
Briseida
Briseis
Briseyda
Brissa
Bristol
Brit
Brita
Brite
Brites
Britney
Britta
Brittany
Brittney
Brixton
Brock
Broderick
Brodie

Bro
Broga.
Broin
Bromley
Bronek
Bronislav
Bronislaw
Bronson
Bronwen
Bronwyn
Brook
Brooke
Brooklyn
Brooklynn
Brooks
Brown
Bruce
Brunhilda
Bruno
Bryan
Bryana
Bryann
Bryanna
Bryanne
Bryant
Bryce
Brycen

Bryden
Brygid
Brylee
Bryn
Brynlee
Brynn
Bryon
Bryony
Bryson
Bssil
Bubba
Buck
Buckley
Bud
Buddy
Budek
Budislav
Buffy
Bunko
Burdette
Burgess
Burke
Burl
Burle
Burne
Burt
Buster

Buttercup
Byron

C

Cabot
Cachamwri
Cadby
Cade
Cadell
Caden
Cadence
Cadman
Cady
Caedmon
Caelan
Caelum
Cagney
Cahal
Cai
Caia
Caiden
Cailyn
Caiman
Cain
Caio
Cairbre
Cairo

Caitlin
Caitlyn
Caius
Calantha
Calanthe
Calder
Caldera
Caldwell
Cale
Caleb
Caledonia
Calendula
Calhoun
Cali
Calia
Calista
Calix
Caliyah
Calla
Callahan
Callaia
Callan
Callen
Callie
Calliope
Callisto
Callum

Calum	Candra
Calvert	Candy
Calvin	Canei
Calypso	Canna
Calytrix	Cannon
Cambria	Canon
Camden	Canton
Camdyn	Canute
Camellia	Canyon
Cameo	Caoilfhinnn
Camero	Caoimhe
Cameron	Caoimhghin
Camey	Cappy
Camila	Capri
Camilla	Car
Camille	Cara
Camilo	Caradoc
Camlin	Caraway
Campbell	Carbry
Campion	Carden
Camron	Cardew
Camryn	Carew
Canaan	Carey
Candace	Carina
Candice	Carissa
Candida	Carl
Candido	Carla

Carleton

Carlie

Carlo

Carlos

Carlotta

Carlton

Carly

Carlyle

Carmel

Carmela

Carmella

Carmelo

Carmen

Carmine

Carnation

Carney

Carol

Carole

Carolina

Caroline

Carolyn

Carr

Carrie

Carrington

Carrol

Carroll

Carson

Carter

Carter / Karter

Caruso

Carvell

Carwyn

Cary

Cascade

Case

Casen

Casey

Cash

Cason

Caspar

Casper

Caspian

Cassandra

Cassava

Cassia

Cassian

Cassidy

Cassie

Cassiopeia

Cassius

Cassivellaunus

Castiel

Castor

Caswallan

Cataleya
Catalina
Catcher
Catena
Caterina
Cathair
Cathal
Cathaoir
Catherine
Cathleen
Cathy
Catkin
Cattaleya
Cattleya
Cave
Cayden
Caydence
Cayenne
Cayla
Caylee
Cayson
Cecelia
Cecil
Cecilia
Cecily
Cedar
Cedric

Celandine
Celeste
Celestia
Celestin
Celia
Celina
Celine
Celyddon
Celyn
Cerdwin
Cereus
Cerise
Cersei
Cesar
Ceslav
Chad
Chadwick
Chaim
Chan
Chana
Chance
Chandler
Chanel
Chanelle
Chaney
Channing
Chara

Charis

Charity

Charlee

Charleigh

Charlene

Charles

Charleston

Charley

Charli

Charlie

Charlie / Charley

Charlize

Charlotte

Chase

Chaya

Chaz

Che

Chelsea

Chelsey

Cheney

Cherish

Cherry

Chester

Chevelle

Chevy

Cheyenne

Chiara

Chiasa

Chieko

Chiharu

Chika

Chikako

Chilton

Chinami

Chitose

Chiyo

Chizu

Chloe

Chloé

Cho

Chris

Chris/Kris

Chrisoula

Christabel

Christian

Christiana

Christina

Christine

Christopher

Christy

Chrysalis

Cian

Ciara

Ciaran

Cici	Clayton
Cielo	Clematis
Cienna	Clemence
Cierra	Clemensia
Cillian	Clement
Cindy	Clementine
Cinnamon	Cleo
Cinnia	Cleome
Cinnie	Cleveland
Circe	Cliantha
Citlali	Cliff
Citlalli	Clifford
Citlaly	Clifton
Citrine	Clint
Citron	Clinton
Claiborne	Clive
Claire	Clodagh
Clancy	Cloud
Clara	Clove
Clare	Clove/Clover
Clarence	Clover
Clarissa	Clust
Clark	Clustfeinad
Clarke	Clyde
Claude	Coalan
Claudia	Cobalt
Clay	Coby

Cocidius
Coco
Codey
Codie
Cody
Cohen
Coinneach
Colbert
Colbie
Colborn
Colby
Cole
Coleman
Colette
Coleus
Colin
Colleen
Collette
Collin
Collins
Colm
Colombine
Colson
Colt
Coltan
Colten
Colter

Colton
Columba
Columbus
Comet
Con
Conal
Conall
Conall Cernach
Conan
Conant
Conchobar
Condan
Condon
Conn
Connal
Connell
Conner
Connie
Connla
Connor
Conor
Conrad
Conroy
Constance
Consuelo
Conway
Cooper

Copper

Cora

Coral

Coralie

Coraline

Corann

Corazon

Corban

Corben

Corbett

Corbin

Cordelia

Cordell

Corey

Corina

Corinna

Corinne

Corliss

Cormac

Cornel

Cornelia

Cornelius

Cortez

Cory

Corymbia

Cosette

Cosima

Cosimo

Cosmo

Cotton

Coty

Coulter

Courtenay

Courtland

Courtney

Cove

Coventina

Covey

Cowan

Cradawg

Crag

Craig

Crane

Crawford

Creed

Creek

Creighton

Creola

Crescent

Cressida

Crevasse

Crew

Cricket

Crisanta

Crispin
Cristal
Cristian
Cristina
Cristopher
Croix
Cromwell
Crosby
Cruz
Crystal
Ctibor
Ctik
Ctirad
Ctislav
Cuchulain
Cuinn
Culain
Culann
Cullen
Currier
Curtis
Custennin
Cuyler
Cyclone
Cygni
Cynthia
Cypress

Cyric
Cyril
Cyrilla
Cyrus

D

Dacey
Dacite
Daenerys
Daffodil
Dafne
Dahlia
Dai
Daichi
Dailyn
Daira
Daire
Daisuke
Daisy
Daitan
Dakari
Dakota
Dakota / Dakotah
Dal
Dalary
Dale
Dalek
Daleyza
Dalia

Daliah
Dalibor
Dalila
Dalilah
Dallas
Dalton
Daman
Damari
Damaris
Damek
Damian
Damien
Damion
Damon
Dan
Dana
Dana / Dane
Danae
Dandelion
Dandre
Dane
Danelly
Dangelo
Dangerfield
Dani
Dania
Danica

Daniel	Darla
Daniela	Darleen
Danielius	Darlene
Daniella	Darlyn
Danielle	Darnell
Danika	Darragh
Daniyal	Darrel
Danna	Darrel /Darryl /Daryl
Danner	Darrell
Danny	Darren
Dante	Darrick
Danu	Darrin
Danyal	Darrius
Daphne	Darryl
Daquan	Darsh
Dara	Daru
Darby	Darwin
Darcy	Darya
Daria	Daryl
Darian	Dash
Dariana	Dasha
Dariel	Dashawn
Darien	Dave
Darin	David
Dario	Davin
Darion	Davina
Darius	Davion

Davis
Davon
Dawid
Dawn
Dawood
Dawson
Dawud
Dax
Daxton
Dayana
Dayanara
Dayanna
Dayra
Dayton
Deacon
Dean
Deandre
Deangelo
Deanna
Dearg
Debora
Deborah
Dechtire
Declan
Dedric
Deen
Deepak

Defne
Deheune
Deidre
Deirdre
Deja
Delaney
Delanie
Delano
Delia
Delilah
Della
Delmore
Delphine
Delta
Delylah
Demarcus
Demelza
Demetria
Demetrius
Demi
Dempsey
Den
Denali
Denham
Denis
Denise
Denisse

Deniz

Dennis

Denver

Denzel

Denzil

Deoch

Deon

Deonte

Derecho

Derek

Derick

Dermot

Derowen

Derrick

Derry

Derya

Desdemona

Deshawn

Desiree

Desmond

Destin

Destinee

Destiny

Deutzia

Dev

Deva

Devan

Devante

Deven

Devin

Devina

Devnet

Devon

Devona

Devonte

Devyn

Dewain

Dewayne

Dewi

Dexter

Dhruv

Diamond

Diana

Diane

Dianella

Dianna

Diantha

Diego

Dierdre

Digby

Diggory

Dilan

Dilbert

Dillan

Dillion

Dillon

Dilys

Dimitri

Dimona

Dina

Dinah

Dinsmore

Dion

Dione

Dior

Dirk

Dita

Diva

Divakar

Divine

Divone

Dixie

Diya

Dobromil

Dobromir

Dobroslav

Doirean

Dolores

Domhnall

Dominic

Dominick

Dominik

Dominique

Dominykas

Don

Donaghy

Donal

Donald

Donall

Donat

Donatella

Donati

Donavan

Donella

Donia

Donna

Donnally

Donnchadh

Donnell

Donnelly

Donnie

Donogb

Donovan

Donte

Dora

Doran

Doreen

Doreena

Dorian

Doris

Dorothea

Dorothy

Dorran

Dorset

Dory

Dosne

Doug

Dougal

Doughal

Doughlas

Dougie

Douglas

Dove

Dover

Doy

Doyle

Draco

Drake

Dream

Dree

Drem

Drever

Drew

Driscol

Driscoll

Driskell

Druce

Drudwyn

Drummond

Duane

Dubv

Dudley

Duer

Duff

Duffey

Duffy

Dughall

Duke

Dulce

Dumin

Duncan

Dune

Dunham

Dunja

Dunley

Dunn

Duran

Durko

Durward

Dusa

Dusan

Dusanek

Dustin
Dusty
Duysek
Dwayne
Dwight
Dyfed
Dylan

E

Ea
Eagan
Eagle
Eamon
Earhart
Earl
Earnest
Eartha
Easterly
Easton
Eastyn
Ebba
Eben
Ebony
Eburscon
Echidna
Eda
Edan
Edana
Edda
Eddie
Eddy
Edelweiss

Eden
Edgar
Edie
Edison
Edith
Edmund
Edna
Edrei
Edsel
Eduardo
Edward
Edwin
Eesa
Efnisien
Efrain
Egan
Egeria
Egerton
Eghan
Eglantine
Egypt
Ehsan
Eibhlín
Eichi
Eike
Eiko
Eila

Eileen	Elena
Eilon	Eleni
Eimy	Elestren
Einion	Elettra
Eira	Elfrida
Eirene	Elgin
Eisa	Elgine
Eisley	Eli
Eithan	Elia
Eiza	Elian
Ekaterina	Eliana
Ela	Elianna
Eladio	Elias
Elaina	Elidor
Elaine	Eliel
Elam	Eliette
Elan	Elif
Elara	Elijah
Elayna	Elin
Elder	Elina
Eldon	Elinor
Eldora	Eliot
Eldoris	Elis
Eldred	Elisa
Eldridge	Elisabeth
Eleanor	Elise
Eleanora	Eliseo

Elisha

Eliska

Elissa

Eliyanah

Eliza

Elizabella

Elizabeth

Elizah

Eljin

Ella

Elle

– Ellen

Ellery

Ellia

Elliana

Ellianna

Ellie

Elliot

Elliot / Elliott

Elliott

Ellis

Ellison

Elly

Elm

Elmer

Elmira

Elmo

Elmore

Elodea

Elodie

Eloisa

Eloise

Elon

Elora

Elowen

Elroy

Elsa

Elsha

Elsie

Elton

Elva

Elvina

Elvira

Elvis

Elwood

Elyana

Elyse

Elysia

Elyssa

Ema

Emani

Emanuel

Emanuele

Emarie

Embelia	Emlyn
Ember	Emma
Emberly	Emmalee
Emelia	Emmaline
Emelie	Emmalyn
Emeline	Emmalynn
Emely	Emmanuel
Emerald	Emmanuelle
Emeri	Emmarie
Emerie	Emmarose
Emerson	Emme
Emersyn	Emmeline
Emery	Emmet
Emery / Emory	⁓ Emmett
Emi	Emmi
Emiko	Emmie
Emil	Emmitt
Emile	Emmy
Emilee	Emory
Emilia	Emre
Emiliana	Emrie
Emiliano	Emry
Emilie	Emrys
Emilio	Ena
Emily	Eneco
Emir	Engl
Emiyo	Enid

Enoch	Erika
Enola	Erin
Enrico	Erina
Enrique	Eris
Ensley	Erity
Enya	Erlina
Enzo	Erlinda
Eoghan	Erma
Eoghann	Ermias
Eoin	Ermine
Eos	Erna
Eowyn	Ernest
Ephraim	Ernestine
Ephron	Ernesto
Equinox	Ernie
Eranthe	Errol
Erasmo	Erskine
Erea	Ervin
Eren	Erwin
Eri	Eryk
Eric	Eryn
Erica	Esa
Erich	Escallonia
Erick	Eshaan
Ericka	Eshan
Erie	Esme
Erik	Esmeralda

Esmond	Eugenie
Esperanza	Euglena
Esteban	Eulalia
Estefania	Eunice
Estefany	Euphemia
Estela	Eva
Estella	Evadne
Estelle	Evalina
Ester	Evalyn
Estevan	Evalynn
Esther	Evan
Estrella	Evangelina
Estuary	Evangeline
Etain	Evanthe
Etana	Eve
Eternity	Evelin
Ethan	Evelina
Ethel	Eveline
Ethne	Evelyn
Etienne	Evelynn
Etsu	Ever
Etsuko	Everard
Etta	Everest
Euan	Everett
Eudora	Evergreen
Eugene	Everlee
Eugenia	Everleigh

Everley
Everly
Evette
Evi
Evie
Evolet
Evonne
Evora
Evza
Evzek
Evzen
Evzenek
Ewald
Ewan
Ewen
Ewyn
Exton
Ezekiel
Ezequiel
Ezra
Ezume

F

Faber
Fabia
Fabian
Fabienne
Fabiola
Fahad
Fainche
Fairfax
Faisal
Faith
Faizaan
Faizan
Falcon
Fallon
Fanousek
Farah
Fardoragh
Farhan
Farica
Faris
Farley
Faron
Farrah

Farran
Farrel
Farrell
Farren
Farrin
Fatima
Fauna
Faustino
Fawn
Faye
Fayola
Fearghus
Feather
Fedelm
Feichin
Felan
Felicia
Felicity
Felipe
Felix
Fen
Fenella
Fennel
Fenton
Ferdinand
Ferehar
Ferghus

Fergus	Finghin
Ferguson	Fingula
Fern	Finian
Fernanda	Finlay
Fernando	Finley
Ferrell	Finn
Ferris	Finnbar
Ffion	Finneen
Fflur	Finnegan
Fiachra	Finnian
Fiacra	Finnin
Fiacre	Finnlay
Fianna	Finnley
Fidel	Finnobarr
Field	Finola
Fielding	Fintan
Fifi	Fiona
Fig	Fionan
Figueroa	Fionn
Filber	Fionnbarr
Filip	Fiora
Finbar	Fioralba
Finch	Fiorella
Findabair	Fiorello
Findlay	Firth
Fineas	Fisher
Fineen	Fitzgerald

Fiynn	Floyd
Fjord	Flyn
Flainn	Flynn
Flanagan	Fogartaigh
Flann	Fogarty
Flanna	Fogerty
Flannagain	Foley
Flannagan	Forbes
Flannan	Ford
Flannery	Forest
Fletcher	Forrest
Fleur	Forsythia
Flinn	Fossa
Flint	Fossil
Floinn	Foster
Floortje	Fox
Flor	Foxglove
Flora	Frana
Florence	Frances
Florent	Francesca
Florentina	Francesco
Florian	Francine
Florida	Francis
Florin	Francis / Frances
Florine	Francisco
Florizel	Franciszek
Flower	Franco

Franek

Frank

Frankie

Franklin

Franky

Franta

Frantik

Frantisek

Fraser

Frazer

Fred

→ Freddie

Freddy

Frederic

Frederick

Fredrick

Freedom

Freesia

→ Freya

Freyja

Frida

Frost

Fuchsia

Fudo

Fujita

Fuller

Fulton

Fumiko

Furman

Fynbar

Fynn

G

Gabriel
Gabriela
Gabriella
Gabrielle
Gadhra
Gael
Gaffney
Gage
Gaia
Gaile
Gaines
Gair
Gala
Galanthus
Galatea
Galaxy
Gale
Galena
Gali
Galilea
Galileah
Galileo
Gall

Gallagher
Galvin
Galvyn
Gannon
Gar
Garance
Gardenia
Gardner
Gareth
Garfield
Garland
Garnet
Garret
Garrett
Garrison
Garry
Gary
Gatlin
Gavin
Gawain
Gelso
Gem
Gema
Gemini
Gemma
Gen
Gene

Gene / Jean	Gia
Genesis	Giacinta
Geneva	Giacomo
Genevie	Giada
Genevieve	Giana
Genki	Giancarlo
Gentry	Gianina
Geoffrey	Gianna
George	Gianni
Georgia	Giavanna
Georgie	Gideon
Georgina	Gigi
Gerald	Gilbert
Geraldine	Gilberto
Geranium	Gilda
Gerard	Gildas
Gerardo	Gilford
Germaine	Gilia
German	Gillian / Jillian
Geronimo	Gilmore
Gert	Gilroy
Gertie	Gin
Gertrude	Gina
Gervase	Ginebra
Gesa	Ginerva
Gethin	Ginessa
Gharial	Ginger

Ginkgo
Gino
Gio
Giovanna
Giovanni
Gisela
Gisele
Giselle
Gisselle
Gitta
Giulia
Giuliana
Giulianna
Giulietta
Gizelle
Glacier
Gladiola
Gladys
Glen
Glen / Glenn
Glenn
Glenna
Glifieu
Gloria
Glory
Glyn
Glynis

Godiva
Golda
Golden
Goldie
Goldman
Gonzalo
Gordon
Goro
Gorsedd
Gower
Grace
Gracelyn
Gracelynn
Gracie
Graciela
Grady
Graham
Gráinne
Grania
Granite
Grant
Granville
Gratia
Gray
Gray / Grey
Graydon
Graysen

Grayson
Grazia
Grecia
Green
Greer
Greg
Gregg
Gregory
Greta
Gretchen
Grettel
Grey
Greyson
Griffin
Griselda
Grove
Grover
Groves
Gruddieu
Guadalupe
Gudrun
Guenevere
Guennola
Guillermo
Guinevere
Gulf
Gull

Gulliver
Gunnar
Gunner
Gunther
Gurnoor
Gus
Gustave
Gustavo
Guy
Gwalchmai
Gwawl
Gwen
Gwendolen
Gwendolin
Gwendolyn
Gweneth
Gwenith
Gwenn
Gwenneth
Gwenyth
Gwenyver
Gwern
Gwernaeh
Gwri
Gwydion
Gwyndolin
Gwyneth

Gwynham
Gwynith
Gwynn

H

Haaris
Hachiro
Hadar
Hadassah
Hadden
Hadi
Hadlee
Hadleigh
Hadley
Hadwin
Hagley
Haiden
Haider
Hail
Hailee
Hailey
Hailie
Haisley
Hajime
Hake
Halbert
Halcyon
– Haley

Hali
Hall
Hallam
Halle
Halley
Hallie
Halo
Halsey
Hamal
Hamilton
Hamish
Hampton
Hamza
Hamzah
Hana
Hanako
Hanan
Haneen
Haniya
Hank
Hanna
Hannah
Hannibal
Hans
Hapuka
Harbor
Hardy

Hari	Haruki
Haris	Harun
Harlan	Haruo
Harland	Harvey
Harlee	Hasan
Harleen	Haseeb
Harleigh	Hashim
Harlem	Haskell
Harley	Hasnain
Harlie	Hassan
Harlow	Hastings
Harlowe	Hattie
Harlyn	Havana
Harman	Havelock
Harmon	Haven
Harmoni	Hawa
Harmony	Hawk
Harold	Hawthorn
Haroon	Hawthorne
Harper	Haya
Harri	Hayami
Harriet	Hayden
Harris	Haydn
Harrison	Hayes
Harry	Haylee
Hart	Hayley
Haru	Haylie

Haywood	Henrik
Hazel	Henry
Hazelton	Henwas
Heath	Herb
Heather	Herbert
Heaven	Herbie
Heavenly	Hercules
Hector	Heriberto
Hedley	Herman
Hedwig	Hermione
Hefeydd	Herne
Heidi	Hero
Heidy	Hertha
Heilyn	Hester
Helen	Heywood
Helena	Hezekiah
Heliodor	Hide
Heliotrope	Hideki
Hellen	Hideko
Hemlock	Hideo
Henbeddestr	Hideyo
Hendrick	Hikaru
Hendrix	Hilario
Henley	Hilda
Henna	Hildegarde
Hennessy	Hill
Henri	Hilliard

Hilton	Horton
Hirkani	Hosanna
Hiro	Hoshi
Hiroki	Hotaru
Hirola	Houston
Hiromi	Howard
Hiroshi	Howl
Hiroyuki	Hoyt
Hisa	Huarwar
Hisano	Hubbell
Hisoka	Hubert
Hobart	Huckleberry
Hodge	Hudson
Hoki	Hueil
Holden	Huey
Hollace	Hugh
Holland	Hugo
Hollis	Hulda
Holly	Hulk
Holmes	Humbert
Homer	Humberto
Honesty	Humphrey
Honey	Humza
Honor	Hunt
Honorius	Hunter
Hope	Huon
Horace	Hurley

Husna
Hussain
Hussein
Hutton
Huw
Huxley
Hyacinth
Hyatt
Hydnora
Hydra
Hydrangea
Hydrilla
Hyrum

I

Iago
Ian
Ianthe
Ianto
Ibex
Ibraheem
Ibrahim
Ichabod
Ichigo
Ida
Idelisa
Idelle
Iden
Idina
Ido
Idra
Idris
Iestyn
Ieuan
Ifan
Ignacio
Igor
Ihsan

Ike
Iker
Iku
Ila
Ilan
Ilana
Ilara
Ileana
Ilene
Iliana
Illiana
Ilona
Iluka
Ilyas
Iman
Imani
Imogen
Imran
Inaaya
Inanna
Inara
Inaya
Inayah
Indi
India
Indiana
Indie

Indigo	Isa
Indri	Isaac
Ine	Isabel
Ines	Isabela
Inez	Isabell
Ingrid	Isabella
Inigo	Isabelle
Inness	Isadora
Innis	Isaiah
Io	Isaias
Ioan	Isao
Iolanthe	Isela
⁓Iona	Isha
Ione	Ishaan
Ira	Ishaq
Ireland	Ishika
Irelynn	Isiah
Irene	Isla
Irie	Isle
- Iris	Ismaeel
Irit	Ismael
Irlanda	Ismail
Irma	Isobel
Irven	Isold
Irvin	Isolda
Irving	Isolde
Irvyn	Israel

Issa
Issac
Italia
Italy
Ito
Itzamara
Itzayana
Itzel
Itzia
Iva
Ivan
Ivana
Ivanka
Ivanna
Ivara
Ives
Ivette
Ivo
Ivor
Ivory
Ivy
Iwan
Ixia
Ixora
Iyla
Izaac
Izaak

Izaan
Izabel
Izabella
Izabelle
Izaiah
Izanagi
Izara
Izel

J

Jabari
Jac
Jacaranda
Jace
Jacey
Jacinda
Jacinta
Jack
Jackeline
Jackie
Jackie / Jaqui
Jacklyn
Jacklynn
Jackson
Jaclyn
– Jacob
Jacoby
Jacqueline
Jacquelyn
Jad
Jada
Jade
Jaden

Jaden /Jayden / Ja
Jadiel
Jadon
Jaeden
Jael
Jaelyn
Jaelynn
Jagger
Jago
Jaguar
Jai
Jaida
Jaiden
Jailyne
⇒ Jaime
Jair
Jairo
Jak
Jakari
Jake
Jakob
Jakub
Jalen
Jaliyah
Jamaal
Jamaica
Jamal

Jamar	Janney
Jamari	Janus
Jamel	Japheth
James	Jaquan
James / Jamie / Jayme	Jaqueline
Jameson	Jared
Jamie	Jaretzy
Jamil	Jarita
Jamila	Jarlath
Jamileth	Jarod
Jamir	Jarom
Jamison	Jaron
Jan	Jarrah
Jana	Jarred
Janae	Jarrell
Jane	Jarrett
Janella	Jarrod
Janelle	Jarvis
Janelly	Jase
Janessa	Jasiah
Janet	Jasleen
Janeth	Jaslene
Janice	Jaslyn
Janie	Jasmin
Janine	Jasmine
Janiyah	Jason
Janna	Jasper

Javier

Javion

Javon

Javor

Jax

Jaxen

Jaxon

Jaxson

Jaxton

Jaxx

Jaxxon

Jay

Jayce

Jaycee

Jayceon

Jaycie

Jayda

Jaydan

Jayde

Jayden

Jayden-lee

Jaydon

Jayla

Jaylah

Jaylani

Jaylee

Jayleen

Jaylen

Jaylene

Jaylie

Jaylin

Jayline

Jaylon

Jaylyn

Jaylynn

Jayne

Jayson

Jazelle

Jaziah

Jaziel

Jazleen

Jazlene

Jazlyn

Jazlynn

Jazmin

Jazmine

Jazmyn

Jazzlyn

Jean

Jeanette

Jedidiah

Jeevan

Jeff

Jefferson

Jeffery	Jesiah
Jeffrey	Jeslyn
Jelena	Jess
Jemima	Jessa
Jemma	Jessamine
Jenelle	Jessamy
Jenesis	Jesse
Jenevieve	Jesse / Jessie
Jenna	Jessi
Jennie	Jessica
Jennifer	Jessie
Jenny	Jesslyn
Jennyfer	Jesus
Jennyver	Jet
Jensen	Jethetha
Jenson	Jethro
Jerald	Jett
Jeremiah	Jewel
Jeremias	Jhene
Jeremy	Jia
Jeriah	Jianna
Jericho	Jillian
Jermaine	Jim
Jerome	Jimena
Jerrod	Jimmie
Jerry	Jimmy
Jeryl	Jin

Jiro
Jiselle
Jiya
Joan
Joana
Joanna
Joanne
Joaquin
Joben
Jocelyn
Jocelyne
Jocelynn
Jody
Joe
Joel
Joelle
Joesph
Joey
Johan
Johana
Johanna
Johannes
John
John-james
Johnathan
Johnathon
Johnnie

Johnny
Joie
Jolee
Jolene
Jolie
Jon
Jonah
Jonas
Jonathan
Jonathon
Jonny
Jonquil
Jonty
Jordan
Jordon
Jordy
Jordyn
Jordynn
Jorge
Jose
Josef
Josefina
Joselin
Joselyn
Joseph
Josephina
Josephine

Josh	Julia
Joshua	Julian
Josiah	Juliana
Josie	Juliane
Joslyn	Julianna
Josselyn	Julianne
Josslyn	Julie
Josue	Julien
Journee	Juliet
Journey	Julieta
Journi	Julieth
Jovan	Julietta
Jovanni	Juliette
Jovie	Julio
Joy	Julissa
Joyce	Julius
Joziah	Jun
Juan	Juna
Juanita	Junaid
Jubilee	June
Judah	Junior
Jude	Juniper
Judith	Junko
Judson	Juno
Judy	Jupiter
Juelz	Jurnee
Jules	Justice

Justin
Justine
Justus

K

Kabir
Kace
Kacey
Kacper
Kade
Kaden
Kadence
Kadin
Kaede
Kaeden
Kaelan
Kaelani
Kaelyn
Kaelynn
Kai
Kaia
Kaidan
Kaiden
Kaidence
Kaie
Kaila
Kailah
Kailani

Kailee
Kailey
Kaily
Kailyn
Kaimana
Kaine
Kaira
Kairi
Kairo
Kaiser
Kaisley
Kaison
Kaitlyn
Kaitlynn
Kaiya
Kaiyo
Kajus
Kalani
Kale
Kalea
Kaleah
Kaleb
Kalel
Kalena
Kaley
Kali
Kalia

Kaliah

Kalila

Kalina

Kaliyah

Kallie

Kallum

Kamal

Kamari

Kamden

Kamdyn

Kameko

Kameron

Kamil

Kamila

Kamilah

Kamilla

Kamille

Kamiyah

Kamran

Kamryn

Kamryn / Camryn

Kana

Kanaye

Kane

Kannon

Kano

Kantuta

Kaori

Kara

Karam

Kareem

Karely

Karen

Kari

Karim

Karina

Karis

Karisma

Karissa

Karl

Karla

Karlee

Karleen

Karley

Karlie

Karma

Karney

Karol

Karolina

Karoline

Karri

Karson

Karsyn

Karter

Kase

Kasen

Kasey

Kash

Kashton

Kason

Kasper

Kassandra

Kassia

Kassiani

Kassidy

Kataleya

Katalina

Katarina

Katashi

Kate

Katelyn

Katelynn

Katerina

Katharine

Katherine

Kathleen

Kathryn

Kathy

Katia

Katie

Katja

Katrina

Katsumi

Katy

Katya

Kauri

Kavya

Kawa

Kay

Kaya

Kayan

Kaycee

Kayden

Kaydence

Kaydon

Kayla

Kaylah

Kaylan

Kaylani

Kaylee

Kayleen

Kayleigh

Kaylen

Kaylene

Kayley

Kayli

Kaylie

Kaylin

Kaylum	Keir
Kaylynn	Keira
Kayne	Keiran
Kaysen	Keiron
Kayson	Keiry
Kazashi	Keith
Keagan	Keith / Keath
Keaghan	Kelby
Keane	Kellan
Keanu	Kellen
Kearney	Kelly
Keary	Kelp
Keaton	Kelsea
Keegan	Kelsey
Keelan	Kelsie
Keeley	Kelton
Keelia	Kelvan
Keelin	Kelven
Keely	Kelvin
Keenan	Kelvyn
Keene	Kelwin
Kegan	Kelwyn
Kehlani	Kemp
Kei	Ken
Keila	Kendal
Keilani	Kendall
Keily	Kendhal

Kendon	Kerrigan
Kendra	Kerry
Kendrick	Kerwin
Kenelm	Kerwyn
Kenia	Keturah
Kenley	Kevan
Kenna	Keven
Kennedi	Kevin
Kennedy	Kevyn
Kennedy / Kennedi	Keyaan
Kenneth	Keyla
Kennocha	Keyon
Kenny	Kezia
Kensington	Keziah
Kensley	Khadija
Kent	Khaleesi
Kentigem	Khalia
Kentigern	Khalid
Kenton	Khalil
Kenya	Khari
Kenyon	Khloe
Kenzie	Kiaan
Kenzo	Kian
Keon	Kiana
Keren	Kianna
Kermit	Kiara
Kermode	Kiera

Kieran	Kirra
Kieron	Kirrily
Kiley	Kirsten
Kilian	Kirwin
Killian	Kirwyn
Kim	Kit
Kim / Kym	Kitty
Kimana	Kizzy
Kimani	Klarissa
Kimber	Knightley
Kimberley	Knoll
Kimberly	Knox
Kimora	Koa
King	Kobe
Kingsley	Kobi
Kingston	Kobie
Kinley	Koby
Kinsey	Koda
Kinslee	Kodi
Kinsley	Kody
Kinzley	Kofi
Kipling	Kohana
Kipp	Kohen
Kira	Kojo
Kiran	Kolby
Kiri	Kole
Kirk	Kolten

Kolton	Krys
Komal	Krzy
Konrad	Kı
Konstantina	Kudu
Kop	Kunsgnos
Kora	Kurt
Korbin	Kurtis
Korey	Kya
Kori	Kyan
Korra	Kyara
Kory	Kye
Kosmo	Kyla
Krew	Kylah
Krill	Kylan
Kris	Kylar
Krish	Kyle
Krisha	Kylee
Kristen	Kyleigh
Kristian	Kylen
Kristin	Kyler
Kristina	Kylian
Kristine	Kylie
Kristofer	Kylin
Kristopher	Kyllion
Kristy	Kylo
Kruze	Kyng
Krystal	Kynlee

Kynthelig
Kyoko
Kyra
Kyran
Kyree
Kyrie
Kyro
Kyron
Kyros
Kyson

L

Laban
Lacey
Lachlan
Lacy
Ladd
Ladislav
Lady
Lagoon
Laguna
Laila
Lailah
Lailani
Lainey
Lairgnen
Laith
Lake
Lamar
Lamont
Lamprey
Lana
Lance
Land
Landen
Landon
Landry
Landyn
Lane
Laney
Lang
Langston
Lani
Laniyah
Lapis
Lapu
Lara
Laramie
Lareina
Larimar
Larissa
Lark
Larkspur
Larry
Latimer
Laura
Lauraine
Laurel
Lauren
Laurence
Laurence / Lawrence
Laurie

Lauryn

Lava

Lavena

Lavender

Lavinia

Lawrence

Lawson

Laya

Layah

Layan

Layla

Laylah

Laylani

Layne

Layton

Lazarus

Lea

Leaf

Leah

Leander

Leandro

Leanna

Leanne

Leda

Ledger

Lee

Lee / Leigh

Leela

Leen

Leena

Legacy

Legend

Legolas

Leia

Leigh

Leighton

Leila

Leilah

Leilani

Leilanie

Leilany

Leith

Lela

Leland

Lemon

Lena

Leni

Lenna

Lennie

Lennon

Lennox

Lenny

Lenore

Leo

Leon

Leona

Leonard

Leonardo

Leonel

Leonidas

Leonie

Leonora

Leopold

Leroy

Lesley

Leslie

Leslie / Lesley

Lesly

Lester

Leticia

Letitia

Levi

Levon

Lewie

Lewis

Lexa

Lexi

Lexie

Leyla

Leylah

Leylani

Leyton

Lia

Liah

Liam

Lian

Liana

Lianna

Libby

Liberty

Libra

Lidia

Liko

Lila

Lilac

Lilah

Lili

Lilia

Lilian

Liliana

Liliane

Lilianna

Lilias

Liliosa

Lilit

Lilith

Lilium

Lillian

Lilliana

Lillianna

Lillie

Lillith

Lilly

Lillyana

Lillyanna

Lilou

Lily

Lilyana

Lilyanna

Lina

Lincoln

Lind

Linda

Linden

Lindsay

Lindsey

Linette

Ling

Linnea

Linnette

Linus

Lionel

Liora

Lir

Lisa

Lisette

Lita

Litton

Litzy

Liu

Liv

Livia

Liya

Liyana

Liz

Liza

Lizar

Lizbeth

Lizeth

Lizette

Llewellyn

Llewelyn

Lloyd

Lluvia

Llyr

Loch

Lochlan

Locke

Logan

Lois

Loki

Lola

London	Lowri
Londyn	Loyalty
Ione	Luana
Lonnie	Luba
Lorcan	Luc
Lorelai	Luca
Lorelei	Lucas
Loren	Lucca
Lorena	Lucero
Lorenzo	Lucia
Loretta	Lucian
Lori	Lucian / Lucy-Ann
Lorna	Luciana
Lorne	Lucianna
Lorraine	Luciano
Lottie	Lucie
Lotus	Lucien
Lou	Lucienne
Loui	Lucille
Louie	Lucinda
~ Louis	Lucius
Louisa	Lucy
Louise	Ludmilla
Lourdes	Luella
Love	Luis
Lovely	Luisa
Lowell	Luka

Lukas

Lukasz

Luke

Lula

Lulu

Lumi

Luna

Lupin

Lupita

Luqman

Luther

Lux

Luxovious

Luz

Lyanna

Lydia

Lyla

Lylah

Lyle

Lyman

Lyndon

Lynet

Lynette

Lynn

Lynx

Lyonesse

_ Lyra

Lyre

Lyric

M

Mab
Mabel
Mabina
Mabon
Mac
Macauley
Maccus
Mace
Macey
Macey/Macy
Maci
Macie
Maciej
Mack
Mackenzie
Macklin
Macklyn
Macon
Macsen
Macy
Mada
Madaio
Madalyn
Madalynn
Madden
Maddie
Maddison
Maddock
Maddox
Madeiran
Madeleine
Madelief
Madeline
Madelyn
Madelyne
Madelynn
Madilyn
Madilynn
Madison
Madisyn
Madyson
Mae
Maeve
Maeveen
Magali
Magaly
Magdalena
Magdalene
Maggie
Magnolia

Magnus

Maha

Mahdi

Mahir

Mahogany

Mahoney

Mai

Maia

Maida

Mailen

Maine

Maira

Maisie

Maison

Maite

Maitland

Maiya

Maize

Majesty

Major

Makai

Makayla

Makena

Makenna

Makenzie

Makepeace

Maksim

Maksymilian

Malachi

Malachy

Malak

Malakai

Malakhi

Malani

Malaya

Malayah

Malaysia

Malcolm

Maleah

Malena

Mali

Malia

Maliah

Malik

Malina

Maliya

Maliyah

Mallory

Malus

Malvin

Malvina

Malvyn

Mamie

Mandrake

Mandy
Maneh
Manfred
Manley
Mannat
Manning
Mannix
Manraj
Mansi
Manuel
Manuka
Manzi
Maple
Mar
Mara
Marbella
Marble
Marc
Marcel
Marcela
Marceline
Marcella
Marcello
Marcellus
Marcelo
Marco
Marcos

Marcus
Marden
Marek
Marella
Marely
Maren
Margaret
Margarita
Margaux
Margo
Margot
Marguerite
Mari
Maria
Mariah
Mariam
Marian
Mariana
Marianna
Marianne
Maribel
Maribelle
Maricela
Marie
Mariel
Mariela
Mariella

Marielle	Marlin
Marigold	Marlo
Marilla	Marlon
Marilyn	Marlow
Marina	Marlowe
Marine	Marmaduke
Mariner	Marques
Marino	Marquis
Mario	Marquise
Marion	Mars
Maris	Marsden
Marisa	Marsh
Marisol	Marshall
Marissa	Martha
Maritza	Martin
Mariyah	Marty
Marjeta	Marvin
Marjoram	Marvina
Marjorie	Marvyn
Mark	Marwa
Markus	Mary
Marla	Maryam
Marlee	Maryjane
Marleigh	Mason
Marlene	Massif
Marley	Matas
Marlie	Mateo

Mateusz	Maximillian
Mather	Maximo
Mathew	Maximus
Mathias	Maxine
Matias	Maxton
Matilda	Maxwell
Matt	May
Matteo	Maya
Matthew	Mayah
Matthias	Mayeli
Mattie	Mayleen
Maude	Maylin
Maura	Maynard
Maureen	Mayo
Maurice	Mayra
Mauricio	Mayson
Mavelle	Mayte
Maven	Mazie
Maverick	Mazzy
Mavie	Mckayla
Mavis	Mckenna
Mawar	Mckenzie
Max	Mckinley
Maxi	Md
Maxim	Mead
Maximilian	Meadghbh
Maximiliano	Meadow

Meadowlark	Melvin
Medb	Melvina
Medredydd	Melvyn
Meera	Memphis
Megan	Menw
Meghan	Mercedes
Mehar	Mercer
Mehmet	Mercury
Mei	Mercy
Meilani	Mere
Mekhi	Meredith
Mekong	Merida
Melani	Meriel
Melania	Merit
Melanie	Meriwether
Melannie	Merlin
Melany	Merlyn
Melia	Merna
Melina	Merrick
Melinda	Merrigan
Melisa	Merrill
Melisende	Merritt
Melissa	Merry
Melodie	Mert
Melody	Merton
Melva	Mervin
Melville	Meryl

Mesa	Mike
Messiah	Mikel
Metztli	Mikey
Mia	Mikhail
Miabella	Mikolaj
Miah	Mila
Mica	Milagro
Micaela	Milagros
Micah	Milah
Michael	Milan
Michaela	Milana
Michal	Milani
Micheal	Milania
Michelangelo	Mileena
Michelle	Milena
Michon	Miles
Michonne	Miley
Mickey	Miliana
Micky	Milla
Migdalia	Millaray
Mignon	Millard
Miguel	Miller
Mika	Millicent
Mikaeel	Millie
Mikaela	Milly
Mikail	Milo
Mikayla	Milosz

Milton	Moana
Mimosa	Modesto
Mina	Mohamad
Minerva	Mohamed
Minka	Mohammad
Minnie	Mohammed
Mira	Mohsin
Mirabella	Moina
Mirabelle	Moira
Miracle	Moises
Mirage	Mollie
Miranda	Molly
Mireya	Mona
Miriam	Monica
Mirna	Monique
Miro	Monroe
Mirta	Monserrat
Mirth	Monserrate
Misael	Monserrath
Misha	Montague
Missy	Montana
Mist	Monte
Misty	Montgomery
Mitchel	Montserrat
Mitchell	Monty
Miya	Moon
Miyah	Mor

Mordechai
Moreen
Morfran
Morgan
Morgana
Morgance
Morgandy
Morgane
Moriah
Morna
Morrigan
Morris
Morrisey
Morton
Morven
Morvyn
Morwenna
Moryn
Moses
Moshe
Moss
Moya
Moyna
Muguet
Muhammad
Muhammed
Mujtaba

Mulberry
Mull
Mungo
Murdoc
Murdoch
Murdock
Muriel
Murphy
Murray
Murry
Murtagh
Musa
Musab
Mustafa
Mya
Myah
Myla
Mylah
Mylene
Myles
Mylo
Mynogan
Myra
Myrna
Myron
Myrthe
Myrtle

N

Nabil
Nadia
Nadine
Nahla
Nahomi
Nahomy
Naia
Naiad
Naila
Nailah
Naim
Naima
Nairn
Nala
Nalani
Naliyah
Nana
Nanala
Nancy
Nanette
Naois
Naomi
Naomy

Naphtali
Napoleon
Nara
Narcissa
Nardos
Nareen
Nareena
Nareene
Nash
Nasir
Nasrin
Natalee
Natalia
Natalie
Nataly
Natalya
Natan
Nataniel
Nataniele
Natasha
Nate
Nathalia
Nathalie
Nathaly
Nathan
Nathanael
Nathanial

Nathaniel	Nelda
Natron	Nell
Nature	Nellie
Nautilus	Nelly
Naveah	Nels
Navy	Nelson
Navya	Nemausus
Naya	Nemertea
Nayeli	Nemi
Nayla	Nemo
Nazayia	Neo
Neal	Nephi
Neala	Neptune
Neale	Neri
Nealie	Nerida
Nealon	Nerissa
Nebula	Nesto
Ned	Nestor
Nedes	Nettie
Neeja	Neva
Neema	Nevada
Neese	Nevaeh
Nefertari	Neveah
Nehemiah	Neville
Neil	Newell
Neill	Newland
Neilson	Newlin

Newlyn	Nikodem
Newman	Nikolai
Ngaio	Nikolas
Nia	Nila
Niall	Nile
Niallan	Nima
Niamh	Nimbus
Nicholas	Nimrod
Nichole	Nina
Nick	Nirvana
Nickolas	Nisien
Nicky	Nita
Nico	Nitella
Nicolas	Nixie
Nicole	Nixon
Nicolette	Niya
Niece	Niyah
Nigel	Noa
Nigella	Noah
Nihal	Noe
Nika	Noel
Nike	Noel / Noelle
Nikhil	Noelani
Nikita	Noelia
Nikki	Noelle
Niklaus	Noemi
Niko	Nohemi

Nojus

Nola

Nolan

Noland

Nona

Noor

Noora

Nora

Norah

Norbert

Noreen

Nori

Norma

Norman

Normand

Normandie

Norris

North

Norton

Norval

Norwood

Nour

Nova

Novah

Novalee

Novia

Noyce

Nuala

Nunatak

Nunzio

Nya

Nyah

Nyimbo

Nyla

Nylah

Nyle

Nyoka

Nyomi

Nyra

Nysa

Nyssa

O

Oak
Oaklee
Oakleigh
Oakley
Oaklyn
Oaklynn
Obadiah
Oberon
Obsession
Obsidian
Ocean
Oceana
Oceane
Oceanus
Octavia
Octavio
Oda
Ode
Odelia
Odessa
Odette
Odin
Odonata

Odyssey
Ofelia
Ogden
Oifa
Oilell
Oisin
Ola
Olaf
Oldrich
Olea
Oleana
Oleander
Oleg
Olga
Olin
Olive
Oliver
Olivia
Olivier
Olivine
Oliwier
Ollie
Olly
Olwen
Olwyn
Olympia
Olympus

Omar	Orlean
Omari	Orman
Omer	Ornelia
Omyra	Ornella
Onda	Orpheus
Ondine	Orquida
Onyx	Orrick
Oona	Orsa
Opal	Orson
Ophelia	Orville
Oprah	Osaka
Ora	Osbert
Orabela	Oscar
Oralie	Osckar
Oran	Osian
Orane	Osiris
Orange	Oskar
Orchid	Osker
Ore	Osman
Oren	Osmond
Oriana	Osvaldo
Oriel	Oswald
Orin	Oswin
Oriole	Othello
Orion	Otis
Orla	Otten
Orlando	Otter

Ottilie
Otto
Ouida
Ove
Ovid
Owain
Owais
Owen
Owin
Owyn
Oxford
Oyintsa
Oz
Ozette
Ozias

P

Pablo
Pacific
Pacifica
Packard
Paddy
Padraig
Paige
Paislee
Paisleigh
Paisley
Paityn
Paizlee
Palash
Palesa
Palma
Palmer
Paloma
Pamela
Pandora
Pangiota
Pangolin
Paniz
Panra

Pansy
Paola
Papatya
Paprika
Parhelion
Paris
Park
Parker
Parr
Parthenia
Parthenope
Pat
Patchouli
Patia
Patience
Patricia
Patrick
Patrik
Patrin
Patryk
Patten
Paul
Paula
Paulette
Paulina
Pauline
Paulo

Pavel	Peridot
Pawel	Perla
Pax	Perre
Paxton	Perry
Payson	Perry / Perrie
Payton	Persephone
Payton / Peyton	Perseus
Pazia	Pert
Peace	Perth
Peach	Petal
Peaches	Pete
Pearl	Peter
Pedro	Petra
Pell	Petros
Pema	Petunia
Penarddun	Peyton
Penelope	Phaedra
Penitentes	Phelan
Penley	Philemon
Penn	Philip
Penny	Philippa
Penthia	Phillip
Peony	Philo
Pepper	Phineas
Percival	Phoebe
Percy	Phoenix
Peregrine	Photinia

Phyllida	Popular
Phyllis	Porter
Phyllon	Portia
Pia	Posey
Picotee	Posy
Piera	Powell
Pierce	Prairie
Pierre	Pranav
Piers	Precious
Pierson	Prentice
Pilar	Preslee
Pilchard	Presley
Pine	Preston
Pinneped	Primrose
Piotr	Primula
Pip	Prince
Piper	Princess
Pippa	Princeton
Piran	Priscila
Pixie	Priscilla
Placido	Prisha
Plum	Priya
Poet	Promise
Polina	Prunella
‒ Polly	Pryderi
Poplar	Ptolemy
‒ Poppy	Putnam

Pwyll

Q

Qasim
Quaid
Quarry
Quartz
Qued
Queen
Queena
Queenie
Quennel
Quentin
Quill
Quin
Quince
Quincy
Quinn
Quinten
Quintin
Quinton

R

Rabbit
Rachael
Rachel
Rada
Radcliff
Radella
Rae
Raees
Raegan
Raelin
Raelyn
Raelynn
Rafael
Rafe
Rafferty
Rafflesia
Ragnar
Raheem
Rahul
Raiden
Raihan
Rain
Raina

Rainbow
Raine
Rainer
Rainey
Rainy
Raisa
Raizel
Raja
Rajan
Rajveer
Raleigh
Ralph
Ralphie
Ralphy
Ramiro
Ramon
Ramona
Ramsey
Randa
Randal
Randall
Randolph
Randy
Ranger
Rania
Ranier
Ransford

Ransley	Rayne / Rain
Ransom	Rayyan
Ranveer	Raz
Raphael	Read
Raquel	Reagan
Rashad	Reaghan
Rasmus	Reba
Raul	Rebeca
Raven	Rebecca
Ravinger	Rebekah
Rawlins	Rebel
Ray	Red
Raya	Redford
Rayaan	Reece
Rayan	Reed
Rayburn	Reef
Rayden	Reegan
Rayen	Reese
Rayhan	Reeve
Raylan	Regan
Rayleen	Reggie
Raylene	Reghan
Raylynn	Regina
Raymond	Reginald
Raymundo	Rehaan
Rayna	Rehan
Rayne	Reid

Reign	Rhonda
Reilly	Rhoswen
Reina	Rhyley
Remi	Rhys
Remington	Ria
Remy	Rian
Rémy	Ricardo
Ren	Rice
Renata	Richard
Rene	Richie
Rene / Renee	Rick
Renee	Rickena
Renesmee	Rickey
Reuben	Ricky
Revel	Rico
Rex	Rider
Rey	Ridge
Reya	Ridley
Reyansh	Ridwan
Reyna	Rigby
Reynaldo	Rigoberto
Reynold	Rihanna
Rhea	Riley
Rhett	Riley / Ryley
Rhiannon	Riley-james
Rhoda	Riley-jay
Rhodes	Rill

Rilla	Rockwell
Rilynn	Rocky
Rina	Roderick
Ringo	Rodman
Rio	Rodney
Riona	Rodolfo
Ripley	Rodrick
Rishi	Rodrigo
Rishley	Rogelio
Rita	Roger
River	Rogue
Rivka	Rohan
Rivulet	Roise
Riya	Roisin
Rizwan	Roland
Roald	Rolando
Roan	Rolf
Robbie	Rollie
Robert	Roma
Roberto	Roman
Robin	Rome
Robin/Robyn	Romeo
Robyn	Romi
Rocco	Romina
Rochester	Romulus
Rocio	Romy
Rock	Ron

Ronald

Ronan

Ronat

Ronin

Ronnie

Ronny

Rorey

Rory

Rosa

Rosabella

Rosalee

Rosalia

Rosalie

Rosalina

Rosalind

Rosalinda

Rosalyn

Rosalynn

Rosamel

Rosamund

Rosanna

Rosario

Rose

Rosella

Roselyn

Roselynn

Rosemarie

Rosemary

Rosen

Roshan

Rosie

Roslyn

Rosmarin

Ross

Rosy

Roux ('Roo')

Rowan

Rowen

Rowena

Rowyn

Roxana

Roxanna

Roxanne

Roxy

Roy

Roya

Royal

Royalty

Royce

Royston

Ruben

Rubi

Rubina

Ruby

Rudi
Rudolph
Rudy
Rudyard
Rue
Rueben
Rufus
Ruhi
Rumi
Rupert
Russell
Rusty
Ruth
Rutherford
Ryan
Ryann
Ryba
Ryder
Rye
Ryker
Rylan
Ryland
Rylee
Ryleigh
Ryley
Rylie
Rylin

S

Saad
Saanvi
Sabella
Sabina
Sabine
Sable
Sabrina
Sachin
Sacrifice
Sade
Sadie
Sadira
Safa
Saffron
Safwan
Sagar
Sage
Sahana
Sahara
Sahasra
Sahib
Sahil
Sai
Saif
Saige
Sailor
Saim
Saint
Saira
Saisha
Sakari
Sakura
Salem
Salil
Salix
Sally
Salma
Salman
Salome
Salton
Salvador
Salvatore
Sam
Sama
Samaira
Samantha
Samanvi
Samar
Samara
Samaya

Sameer

Sami

Samir

Samira

Samiyah

Sammy

Samphire

Samson

Samuel

Samuele

Sana

Sanaya

Sanders

Sandon

Sandra

Sandy

Sanford

Sanidine

Saniyah

Sanna

Sanne

Santana

Santiago

Santino

Santo

Santos

Sanvi

Saoirse

Saoloa

Sapphira

Sapphire

Sara

Sarah

Sarahi

Sarai

Saraid

Saray

Sargassum

Sariah

Sarina

Sariyah

Sascha

Sasha

Saskia

Sativola

Saul

Savanna

Savannah

Savina

Sawyer

Sayed

Saylor

Sayuri

Scarlet

Scarlett
Scarlette
Schuyler
Scilti
Scoria
Scott
Scottie
Scotty
Scout
Sea
Seabert
Seamus
Sean
Seanna
Season
Seb
Sebastian
Sebastien
Sedona
Seerat
Sehaj
Sekani
Selah
Selby
Selena
Selene
Selina

Selma
Senan
Seneca
Senna
Sephora
Sequoia
Sequoyah
Serafina
Seraphina
Serena
Serene
Serenity
Sergio
Serina
Serval
Setanta
Seth
Seven
Sevyn
Seward
Shaan
Shade
Shadow
Shadrack
Shae
Shaelyn
Shah

Shaila
Shaina
Shale
Shanaya
Shane
Shanna
Shannon
Sharon
Shaula
Shaun
Shauna
Shaurya
Shaw
Shawn
Shay
Shayaan
Shayan
Shayla
Shayna
Shayne
Shea
Sheena
Sheikh
Sheila
Shela
Shelby
Sheldon

Shell
Shelley
Shepherd
Sheridan
Sherlock
Sherlyn
Sherman
Sherpa
Sherry
Sherwood
Shiloh
Shipley
Shira
Shirley
Shiv
Shona
Shore
Shoshana
Shreya
Shriya
Shyla
Shylah
Sia
Siana
Sibyl
Sicily
Sid

Siddel
Sidney
Siena
Sienna
Sierra
Sigal
Sigmund
Silas
Silver
Silvia
Simeon
Simon
Simone
Simran
Sincere
Sinéad
Siobhan
Sion
Sipho
Sire
Sireli
Siren
Sirena
Siria
Sirius
Sitara
Siya

Skarlett
Skeet
Skipper
Sky
Sky/Skye
Skye
Skyla
Skylah
Skylar
Skyler
Skyler / Skylar
Slade
Slate
Sloan
Sloan / Slone
Sloane
Snow
Snowden
Snowdrop
Snowy
Socorro
Sofia
Sofie
Sojourner
Sol
Solana
Solange

Solaris	Spruce
Soledad	Sri
Soleil	Stacey
Solomon	Stacy
Solstice	Stanislaw
Solveig	Stanley
Soma	Star
Sona	Starla
Sonia	Starlight
Sonja	Starling
Sonnie	Stefan
Sonny	Steffan
Sonora	Stella
Sonya	Stephan
Sophia	Stephanie
Sophie	Stephany
Sophronia	Stephen
Sora	Stephon
Soraya	Sterling
Sorcha	Sterling / Stirling
Soren	Sterne
Sorrel	Stetson
Sparrow	Steve
Speck	Steven
Spencer	Stevie
Spike	Stewart
Spring	Stockard

Stokley
Stone
Storm
Stormy
Stratus
Strawberry
Stream
Stroud
Stuart
Studs
Sturgeon
Subhaan
Subhan
Success
Sufyan
Sugn
Suhani
Sulaiman
Sulayman
Sullivan
Summer
Summit
Sunny
Sunshine
Suri
Susan
Susana

Susanna
Susannah
Susie
Sutton
Suzanne
Suzette
Suzu
Svaty Vavrinec
Swain
Swan
Swara
Sycamore
Sydney
Sydney / Sidney
Syed
Sylas
Sylvan
Sylvester
Sylvia
Sylvie
Symphony
Szymon

T

Tabitha
Tadc
Tadeo
Tadhg
Taha
Tahlia
Tai
Taima
Taine
Taj
Tajsa
Takashi
Takoda
Tala
Talbot
Talha
Talia
Taliesin
Taliyah
Tallulah
Talon
Talya
Tamala
Tamar
Tamara
Tamarind
Tamarisk
Tamia
Tamir
Tammy
Tancy
Tanguy
Tania
Tanis
Tanner
Tansy
Tanvi
Tanya
Tao
Tara
Taran
Taras
Tarek
Tarian
Tariq
Tarn
Tarragon
Tarun
Taryn
Tatanka

Tate	Teithi
Tatiana	Temperance
Tatum	Tempest
Tatyana	Tenley
Taurean	Tennessee
Taurus	Tennyson
Tavares	Terence
Tave	Teresa
Tavish	Teri / Terry
Tavor	Terra
Tawny	Terran
Taya	Terrance
Taylan	Terrel
Taylen	Terrell
Taylor	Terrence
Tea	Terry
Teagan	Tesla
Teaghue	Tess
Teague	Tessa
Teal	Tetsu
Tecla	Tevin
Ted	Tex
Teddie	Texas
Teddy	Teyrnon
Teegan	Thabo
Tegan	Thaddeus
Tehile	Thais

Thalassa	Thyme
Thalia	Tia
Thallo	Tiago
Thandie	Tiana
Thane	Tianna
Thatcher	Tiara
Thea	Tiberius
Thebe	Tibor
Theirry	Tide
Thelonious	Tiernan
Theo	Tiernay
Theodora	Tierney
Theodore	Tiffany
Theophile	Tigerlily
Theresa	Tiggy
Thetis	Tilly
Thiago	Tim
Thisbe	Timber
Thistle	Timmy
Thomas	Timothy
Thomasina	Tina
Thor	Tinley
Thora	Tinsley
Thorn	Tirzah
Thorne	Titan
Thorpe	Titania
Thurlow	Titus

Tobias	Trace
Tobin	Tracy
Toby	Trahern
Toby / Tobey	Tranter
Todd	Travis
Tom	Travon
Tomas	Treasa
Tomasz	Treasure
Tomkin	Tree
Tommie	Tremaine
Tommy	Tremayne
Tommy-lee	Trent
Tomos	Trenton
Toni	Treva
Tonneau	Trevon
Tony	Trevor
Tony / Toni	Trey
Topaz	Trinity
Tor	Tripp
Tori	Tris
Torin	Trisha
Torrey	Tristan
Tory	Tristen
Tory / Tori	Tristian
Tostig	Tristin
Townsend	Triston
Toyon	Tristram

Triton
Triumphant
Trixie
Troy
Tru
Tru/True
Trudy
Truman
Trystan
Tuatara
Tucker
Tudor
Tulip
Tullia
Tunder
Tupelo
Turi
Turner
Turquoise
Twain
Twilight
Twyla
Ty
Tye
Tyler
Tyler-james
Tyler-jay

Tylor
Tymon
Tymoteusz
Tyne
Typhoon
Tyra
Tyree
Tyrell
Tyrese
Tyron
Tyrone
Tyson
Tzipporah

U

Uberto
Udath
Udaya
Udell
Udo
Ugo
Ula
Ulf
Ulises
Ulrich
Ulrika
Ultan
Ulysses
Uma
Umair
Umar
Umber
Umbra
Una
Undine
Unice
Unique
Unity
Unwyn
Upton
Urban
Urho
Uri
Uriah
Uriel
Uriela
Urien
Urja
Ursa
Ursula
Usher
Usman
Uta
Uttam
Uzair
Uzi

V

Vaclav
Vada
Vadim
Val
Valdemar
Valdis
Vale
Valencia
Valente
Valentin
Valentina
Valentine
Valentino
Valeria
Valerie
Valerio
Valery
Valia
Valkyrie
Valley
Van
Vana
Vance

Vandana
Vanellope
Vanessa
Vanetta
Vangelis
Vania
Vanity
Vanna
Vanya
Vaquita
Varda
Varden
Vardon
Varney
Varro
Varsha
Varun
Varvana
Vashti
Vaughan
Vaughn
Vavrin
Vavrinec
Vayda
Veda
Veer
Vega

Vela	Vianey
Velda	Vianna
Vella	Vianney
Velma	Vibol
Velvet	Vicenta
Venetia	Vicente
Venice	Vick
Venus	Vicky
Vera	Victor
Verbena	Victoria
Verda	Victory
Vered	Vicus
Verena	Vida
Verity	Vidal
Verna	Vidya
Vernell	Vienna
Verner	Vigdis
Vernon	Vihaan
Verona	Vijay
Veronica	Vikram
Versilius	Viktor
Veruca	Viktoria
Vesa	Ville
Vesper	Vina
Vesta	Vincent
Vester	Vincenzo
Vevina	Vine

Vinnie

Vinny

Viola

Violet

Violeta

Violett

Violetta

Violette

Virga

Virgil

Virgile

Virginia

Viridiana

Visara

Vita

Vito

Vittoria

Vittorio

Vitus

Viva

Vivaan

Viveca

Vivek

Vivian

Viviana

Vivianna

Vivianne

Vivien

Vivienne

Vladimir

Volker

Von

Vonda

Voss

W

Wade
Wakefield
Waldemar
Walden
Waldo
Waleed
Waleska
Walker
Wallace
Wallis
Wallis / Wallace
Walta
Walter
Walton
Wanda
Waneta
Ward
Wardell
Warner
Warren
Warwick
Washington
Wasim

Wassily
Watson
Wava
Waverley
Waverly
Wayland
Waylon
Wayne
Webster
Wednesday
Weldon
Wells
Wendell
Wendy
Werner
Werther
Wes
Wesley
Wesson
West
Westin
Westley
Weston
Wetherby
Weylin
Weylyn
Wharton

Wheaton	Willis
Wheeler	Willoughby
Whisper	Willow
Whit	Wilma
Whitfield	Wilmer
Whitley	Wilson
Whitman	Wilton
Whitney	Windsor
Wiktor	Windy
Wilber	Winifred
Wilbur	Winika
Wilda	Winn / Wynn
Wilder	Winnie
Wildflower	Winola
Wildon	Winslow
Wiley	Winston
Wilford	Winter
Wilfred	Winthrop
Wilfreda	Winton
Wilfredo	Wisdom
Wilhelm	Wistan
Wilhelmina	Wisteria
Wilkes	Wittan
Will	Wojciech
Willa	Wolf
William	Wolfe
Willie	Wolfgang

Wolfrom
Wolter
Woodburn
Woodrow
Woodward
Woody
Worcester
Worth
Wrasse
Wren
Wright
Wyatt
Wyclef
Wylie
Wynda
Wyndam
Wynn
Wynne
Wynnie
Wynter

X

Xadrian
Xanadu
Xander
Xannon
Xanthe
Xanthippe
Xanthus
Xaverie
Xavier
Xen
Xena
Xenon
Xerxes
Xeven
Ximena
Ximenna
Xiomara
Xiphia
Xiphosura
Xitlali
Xitlaly
Xiu
Xoan

Xochitl
Xoey
Xristina
Xylander
Xylia
Xzavier

Y

Yaal
Yadid
Yadiel
Yadira
Yadon
Yael
Yaelle
Yaffa
Yahaira
Yahir
Yaholo
Yahya
Yair
Yakiya
Yale
Yamila
Yamilet
Yamileth
Yana
Yaneli
Yangtze
Yanha
Yanira

Yanis
Yann
Yaqub
Yara
Yarden
Yareli
Yarely
Yaretzi
Yaretzy
Yaritza
Yarrow
Yaseen
Yash
Yasin
Yasir
Yasmeen
Yasmin
Yasmine
Yatzil
Yatziri
Yazmin
Ye
Yehuda
Yelena
Yeraldina
Yered
Yerik

Yerodin
Yervant
Yesenia
Yetta
Yeva
Yi
Yisroel
Yitzak
Ylva
Ynyr
Yobachi
Yogi
Yoki
Yolanda
Yoloti
Yona
York
Yosef
Yoselin
Yoselyn
Yoshiko
Yousef
Yousif
Yousuf
Yovela
Ysabel
Ysabella

Ysanne
Yseult
Yspaddaden
Yu
Yuki
Yuliana
Yulissa
Yuna
Yunus
Yurani
Yuri
Yuridia
Yuritzi
Yusef
Yusia
Yusra
Yusuf
Yuuta
Yuvraj
Yves
Yvette
Yvonne

Z

Zac
Zach
Zachariah
Zachary
Zachery
Zack
Zackary
Zackery
Zad
Zada
Zadie
Zadok
Zador
Zafar
Zafira
Zahara
Zahir
Zahra
Zaid
Zaida
Zaide
Zaiden
Zain
Zaina

Zainab
Zaine
Zaira
Zaire
Zak
Zakai
Zakaria
Zakariya
Zakariyya
Zakary
Zaki
Zaley
Zalie
Zamira
Zander
Zane
Zaneta
Zaniyah
Zara
Zarah
Zarek
Zaria
Zariah
Zariyah
Zavier
Zaya
Zayaan

Zayan

Zayd

Zayda

Zayden

Zayla

Zaylee

Zayn

Zayna

Zaynab

Zayne

Zayra

Zdenek

Zdenka

Zebedee

Zebulon

Zechariah

Zee

Zeeshan

Zeina

Zeke

Zelda

Zelenka

Zelia

Zella

Zelma

Zemira

Zena

Zenaida

Zendaya

Zenevieva

Zenith

Zenobia

Zephyr

Zeren

Zeta

Zetta

Zia

Zikani

Zinaida

Zinerva

Zinnia

Zion

Zipporah

Zircon

Zita

Ziva

Ziya

Zoe

Zoey

Zoie

Zola

Zooey

Zora

Zoraida

Zorina
Zosia
Zoya
Zula
Zuleika
Zulema
Zuleyka
Zulma
Zuma
Zumar
Zuri
Zuzana
Zuzu
Zyaire
Zyana
Zyanya
Zyla
Zyon

The   End

Printed in Great Britain
by Amazon

19860367R00092